D0664430

simply™

handwriting
analysis

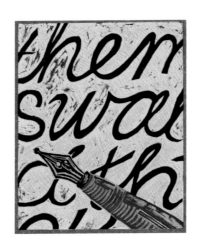

simply™

handwriting
analysis

EVE BINGHAM

WILLIAMSBURG REGIONAL LIBRARY
7770 CROAKER ROAD
WILLIAMSBURG, VIRGINIA 23188

A Sterling / Zambezi Book

Sterling Publishing Co., Inc.

New York

SEP   2007

Library of Congress Cataloging-in-Publication Data Available

2 4 6 8 10 9 7 5 3 1

Published in 2007 by Sterling Publishing Co., Inc.
387 Park Avenue South, New York, NY 10016
Copyright © 2007 by Eve Bingham
Published in the UK solely by Zambezi Publishing Ltd
P.O. Box 221, Plymouth, Devon, PL2 2YJ UK
Distributed in Canada by Sterling Publishing
^{c}/o Canadian Manda Group, 165 Dufferin Street
Toronto, Ontario, Canada M6K 3H6
Distributed in the United Kingdom by GMC Distribution Services
Castle Place, 166 High Street, Lewes,
East Sussex, England BN7 1XU
Distributed in Australia by Capricorn Link (Australia) Pty. Ltd.
P.O. Box 704, Windsor, NSW 2756, Australia

Printed in China
All rights reserved

Sterling ISBN-13: 978-1-4027-4001-5
ISBN-10: 1-4027-4001-8
Zambezi ISBN-13: 978-1-903065-53-2
ISBN-10: 1-903065-53-4

For information about custom editions, special sales, premium
and corporate purchases, please contact Sterling Special Sales
Department at 800-805-5489 or specialsales@sterlingpub.com.

dedication

I dedicate this book to my husband, Dave, for the culinary delights and the numerous cups of tea, and to my sister Val. Extra special thanks to Val for all her grammatical expertise—which was much appreciated.

contents

about the author

Eve Bingham was born Evelyn Rose Curtis in the east end of London, the fifth of six children. She prefers to be called Eve. She is married and has five sons. Eve has always had an interest in what is now termed the New Age arts, and in the early 1970s she became active in her specialized subjects: tarot, numerology, graphology, spiritual development, relaxation, and meditation. She joined the British Astrological and Psychic Society (BAPS) in early 1978, and she represented the society at many New Age festivals and exhibitions. At the same time, she also served many of the spiritualist churches in Britain. She became active on the National Executive Committee of BAPS in the early 1980s and has been involved with the society for the best part of twenty-five years; she currently holds the positions of secretary and company secretary.

introduction

When we were very young children, we were encouraged to draw and color pictures, but the first time we held a pencil or crayon in our hands it felt awkward and rather strange. With continued use we became more adept, but it was only when we arrived at nursery or elementary school that we were taught how to draw a picture and then sign our names at the bottom of it, usually in capital letters.

Child's drawing, signed

Today, our children are encouraged to develop hand-eye coordination, and most of them are able to read and write their own names by the time they reach elementary school. As the years go by, their own unique expression of writing develops. Over time, and with the encouragement of their teachers, their writing becomes more practiced. Most children are taught to write in a similar way, but by the time they reach the age of about twelve years, they choose to vary their writing style in accordance with their unique personalities. From that time on, their signatures become expressions of who they are.

The study of handwriting is referred to as *graphology*. Handwriting can also be regarded as "brain writing." It is an expressive action that reveals the whole personality; each mark on the page contains meanings that a graphologist can interpret. By the time adulthood arrives, all our experiences—the untold twists and turns, ups and downs, highs and lows of life—are reflected in our handwriting. The overall presence of a writing sample on a plain piece of paper can denote a person's unique and individual expression of the inner self. However, while there are many traits we can identify through handwriting analysis, and many ways to identify those traits, keep in mind that it is not possible to identify the gender of an individual from a handwriting sample, or to use graphology to predict the future.

Before you begin to explore this stimulating subject, it would be helpful to collect several handwriting samples from friends and family. Just a few words positioned on a piece of paper, greeting card, or envelope will portray quite a lot about the writer of those words. Collect as many as possible, and with some practice, you will be amazed by what can be revealed.

Different writing characteristics are called "handwriting indicators" or "writing traits." The many script samples in this book include examples of size, slant, pressure, baseline, connection of letters and words, margins on the page and envelope, the three zones, and the signature.

Nowadays, many companies use graphology as an unbiased tool to determine a job applicant's suitability, making handwriting analysis an effective, profitable, and legal means of screening employees. To many, graphology is on par with fortune telling, but some of the largest corporations take it seriously enough to request that job applicants apply in their own handwriting.

Throughout the ages, humanity's method of communication has been primarily in the form of the written word—letters, notes, postcards, lists, reminders, and maybe even a daily diary. Nowadays, however, we rely heavily on technology—computers, cell phones, and so on—to communicate instantly with one another. This is particularly obvious among the members of the younger generation, who, it seems, rarely put pen to paper.

Our handwriting is the product of mind and body because it is composed of thoughts expressed on paper, with the physical movements controlled by the brain but using the muscles of the arm and hand. These movements are influenced by our feelings—our moods, emotions, and reactions to whatever is going on in our lives at that time. Whether we are depressed or worried, have feelings of optimism, anger, or elation, they all have a bearing on the way we write. Our innermost personality is shown on the page at the time of writing.

Whereas a person's handwriting represents the way he or she feels inside, a person's signature represents the public image that the writer wants to project. A wide variation between a person's writing and his or her signature indicates a big difference between the private and public selves. When the writing and the signature are identical, then "what you see is what you get."

An ideal writing sample should be written spontaneously, in ink, on unlined paper, and should be signed by the writer. A sentence or two with a signature, or sometimes a signature alone, can be sufficient for the purposes of analysis if there are enough letters within the sample. A considerable amount of handwriting analysis is common sense. For instance, people who dot their *i*'s and cross their *t*'s precisely tend to be more meticulous than those who do not. Stylish people often have very stylish writing, and so on. Much of what you learn in handwriting analysis will not surprise you at all. The more you learn about graphology, the more you will learn about your friends and family.

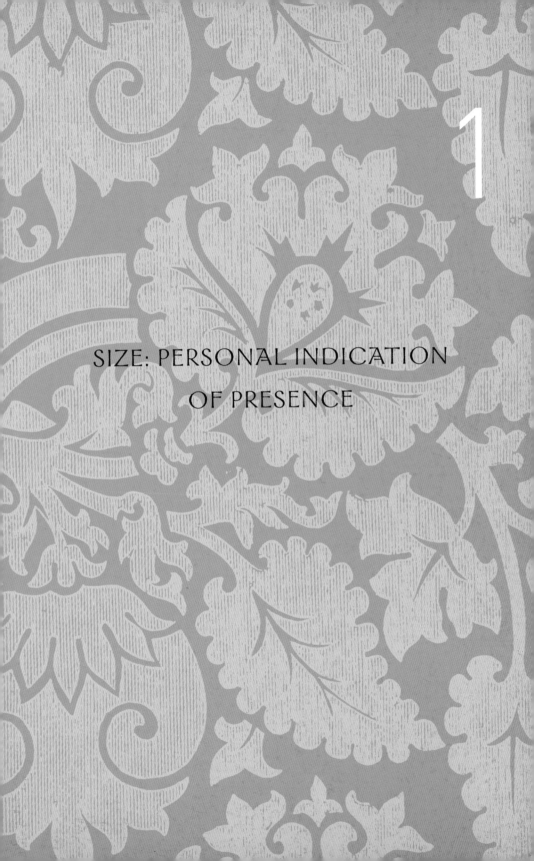

1

SIZE: PERSONAL INDICATION
OF PRESENCE

The size of the script is the first thing we will look at. There are basically three different sizes of script—large, medium, and small—but I have also included a discussion of very small script. Size of script expresses personal self-esteem, self-confidence, and adaptability to other people. Varying sizes within the same script indicate that the writer can be inconsistent and rather erratic.

The size of handwriting in graphology is important, for it reveals how he or she feels about and interacts with family and friends. The size of the writing is one indication of how much the writer wants to be noticed in much the same way that clothing style and color does. When we look at what people are wearing, we assume that someone wearing bold colors wants to be noticed more than someone who chooses to wear neutral tones.

Usually the first thing we notice about someone's handwriting is the size, especially if it is particularly large or small. Just knowing the sample's size opens up an insight into the writer's personality.

LARGE WRITING

and the new year in

Large handwriting

People whose writing is large tend to stand out in a crowd. They like to be noticed and thrive on being the center of attention. These people are ambitious and confident, they tend to have a broad perspective on life, and they can make an impression on everyone they meet. They are bold individuals, driven by their egos. In handwriting, large, bold writing typically says, "Notice me!" People with large handwriting may be those in the public eye, such as politicians, television personalities, pop stars, and actors.

Some positive keywords

active

adventurous

good self-esteem

possibly overgenerous

self-confident

self-reliant

Individuals with large handwriting can have great organizational skills and can show courage and a strong character. They do things on a grand scale but they are not good at handling details.

Some negative keywords

arrogant

boastful

conceited

easily distracted

extravagance

insensitive to others

lack of self-discipline

poor observation

possibly accident-prone

vague, nebulous concepts

MEDIUM-SIZE, OR NORMAL, WRITING

Something else, but

Medium writing

Those individuals whose writing is medium-size, or normal, are flexible and adaptable. These practical, realistic, and balanced people can work well on their own or with others; they can be team leaders or team players and have strong organizational skills. A writer of this type might be found in a large company as the office manager, plodding away with repetitive work but still having the ability to monitor the activities in the rest of the office. People with medium-size writing tend to have a sensible approach to life, know how to keep a balance between work and play, are well liked in their working environment, and have many friends.

Some positive keywords

adaptable

caring

flexible

good judgment

practical

sensible

sociable

trustworthy

Some negative keywords

judgmental

nosy

overfriendly

pedantic tendencies

SMALL WRITING

for your reply. Thankyou.

Small writing

People with small handwriting tend to be objective in their outlook. They are usually private individuals who avoid the limelight and keep very much in the background. These are people who use their brains rather than their brawn. People with small handwriting have a tendency to analyze every-thing, including their own thoughts and feelings.

Some positive keywords

maturity

prudence

realism

Some negative keywords

feelings of inferiority

inhibition

self-limitation

VERY SMALL WRITING

a full recovery

Very small writing

Tiny writing is associated with very intelligent people who intellectualize most things. These modest, humble people can be introverted, but they have good concentration skills. Very small, cramped handwriting can reveal an inferiority complex. People with very small handwriting are introspective and do not seek attention for themselves; they value their privacy more than anything else, and being of an introverted nature, they find it hard to interact with groups of people. An individual with very small handwriting is hiding his or her personality behind a facade of caution and reserve; this person is not interested in an active social life and can be discriminating when choosing close friends and associates.

Some positive keywords

can concentrate

accurate

modest

Some negative keywords

limited interests

little creative imagination

pedantic

self-inflicted isolation

submissive

temporary depression

Some doctors have such small handwriting that it is practically illegible. Scientists, researchers, and mathematicians, and also those who are dealing with facts and figures, are normally found to have very small writing.

2

THE PRESENCE ON THE PAGE

MARGINS ON PAPER

Margins are like the framework of a picture; in this case, the handwriting is the picture. Margins are not consciously made. These spaces show the influence that time and the experience of life has had on the writer.

The Left-Hand Margin

Left-hand margin

The left-hand margin denotes the writer's past influences and the way he or she uses resources. No left-hand margin suggests that the writer lacks self-confidence and could be clinging to the past. It indicates an insecure individual who still suffers in some way from childhood fears or is badly influenced by his past experiences. People who leave no left-hand margin are afraid of being influenced by others and they can overreact to any kind of criticism or change. A very wide left-hand margin can denote a writer who is generous and reserved but it can also mean that the writer can be thrifty but also wants to be popular.

Sometimes, if the script has been written quickly, the left-hand margin gets progressively larger, with the writing starting farther to the right with each line. People who write like this are impulsive, and this trait can indicate an excitable writer who rushes ahead when starting something new, for example, an enjoyable project, a new relationship, or a vacation. This trait can also indicate that the writer is losing control over his or her finances. Sometimes, however, the writer will become aware of this tendency and try to rectify this trait by starting the next paragraph back on track.

The Right-Hand Margin

Some irregularity in the right-hand margin is natural; the writer must decide whether, at the end of a line, the next word will actually fit into the remaining space or whether he or she should divide the word in two using a hyphen. Planning ability, or the absence thereof, is reflected here. Those who have had secretarial or office training will probably control the use of their margins as they would when using a typewriter.

Right-hand margin

Writers who rush to the edge of the paper and leave no margin at all, can be uninhibited and involved with everything and everybody around them. They probably have no fear of the future, meeting it head-on. The person who leaves a wide right margin possibly fears the future, but this trait can also demonstrate artistic abilities, particularly if the right margin is the same size all the way down the page.

All-Around Wide Margins

People who present their writing with clear equally spaced margins all around are those who wish to be clearly understood. They may have a commercial background with an aesthetic sense; possibly they are sensitive individuals who like to use artistic license. If the space is very large, the writer can almost be a recluse.

Writing with all-around wide margins

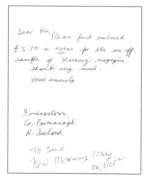

Writing with no margins

No Margins at All

Individuals who leave no margins around their writing can be economical and thrifty to the point of meanness. This trait can also show that the writer has no artistic sense. An individual with this tendency may have a gregarious nature and a need to be loved and wanted; he or she may be a compulsive talker who lacks tact and diplomacy. This writer can cling to past relationships and be unable to let go of past hurts.

Writing with narrow upper margin

Narrow Upper Margin

Writers who use narrow or no upper margins can show a dislike of formality and a lack of respect; this characteristic can also indicate ambition. Writers who use a narrow upper margin display little or no planning skills. They can be pessimistic individuals with little or no artistic abilities; they may have a poor educational background. Young people often use narrow upper margins.

Writing with wide upper margin

Large or Wide Upper Margin

A wide margin left at the top of the page can indicate that the writer has low self-esteem. They may be overly respectful towards their employers and elders. They tend to live in the present and may have little thought for the future.

THE ENVELOPE LAYOUT MARGINS

The envelope is divided into four areas: upper, lower, right, and left.

The Address Written in the Center of the Envelope

Envelope with writing in the center

Writers who place the address in the center of the envelope indicate that they are clear thinkers with the ability to organize. This positioning can also indicate that they are orderly, caring, and considerate of others. Underlined words or phrases show that the writer is fussy and easily worried.

The Address Written to the Far Right of the Envelope

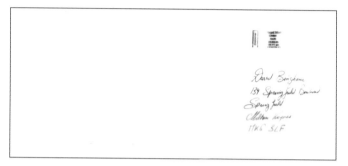

Envelope with address positioned to far right

An address positioned to the far right of the envelope, sometimes with heavy pressure of the script, can indicate an impulsive person who has aggressive tendencies but who also needs the company of others.

The Address Written at the Top of the Envelope

Envelope with address positioned at the top

The placing of the address at the top of the envelope denotes that the writer is enterprising and has the need to express his or her opinions. If only the upper half of the envelope is used, the writer can be immature and prone to daydreaming. Sometimes, a young person who forgets that an area for the stamp needs to be left open writes like this.

The Address Written Very Low, in the Center or Left Position on the Envelope

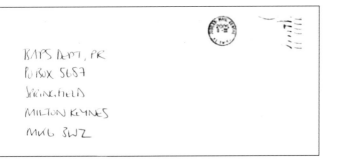

Envelope with address positioned low to the left

An address in an extremely low position, whether it is placed centrally or to the left on the envelope, can indicate anxiety and a pessimistic outlook on life. This positioning can also show a materialistic streak.

No Space Around the Address

Envelope with no space around the address

The writer who leaves no space on the envelope shows a need to participate in all aspects of life. Usually, the writing is extremely large, indicating a person who tends to want to be noticed.

The Address Written to the Left and in the Center of the Envelope

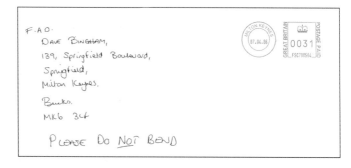

Envelope with address positioned to left and center

The individual who addresses an envelope to the left, centered vertically, can be afraid of life and may also be reserved. This person's interests are more with inanimate objects than with people.

The Address Written in the Bottom Left-Hand Corner

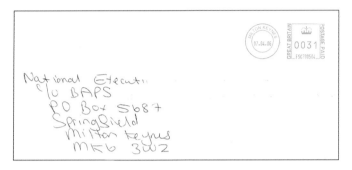

Envelope with address positioned at bottom

Placement of the address in the bottom left-hand corner of the envelope is unusual, but those who do position it here may have very small writing, showing a lack of confidence and an inner need for security.

The Address Written in the Upper Left-Hand Corner

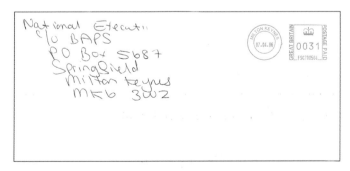

Envelope with addressed positioned at upper left

An address placed in the upper left-hand corner of the envelope denotes a writer who can be an intellectual but is very much a loner.

The Address Written on the Envelope Is Staggered

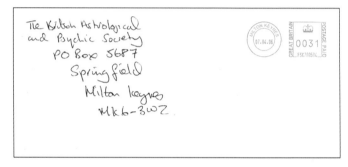

Envelope with address staggered from left top to right bottom

A person who has staggered the address, progressing from the top left to the bottom right, has a cautious and inhibited nature.

The Address Is Extremely Small and in the Center

Envelope with address written very small and positioned in center

An address placed in the center and written extremely small indicates that the writer puts his or her own needs before those of others.

3

SLANTS: THE EMOTIONAL INTERACTIONS

It is important to remember that the more indications you discover in a person's handwriting, and the longer the writing sample is, the better you will understand the writer. There are three basic slants to hand-writing: the right-handed and left-handed slants and the upright slant. On occasion you may find a mixture of these. A graphologist friend of mine has a novel way of remembering the slant indicators: Imagine three people who want a cup of tea. The writer with the left-hand slant would make everyone a cup of tea, the writer with the upright slant would make him- or herself a cup of tea, and the writer with the right-hand slant would delegate someone else to make the tea. We will now look at the various slants in handwriting and see what the differences indicate.

THE RIGHT SLANT

Could you please forward me a list my Surrounding area, as I would

Right-handed slant

The right-handed slant is found in the majority of people's handwriting. This most common slant can show a forward-looking person with a friendly disposition who enjoys human contact and who likes to be surrounded by others. People who display this characteristic have well-developed social instincts and may forget themselves in their interactions with others. These people are sociable and responsive, with good coping abilities. They can be demonstrative and like to show their feelings. The person with a right-handed slant can be extroverted, outgoing, and friendly, and has forward-thinking spontaneity and enthusiasm.

An exaggerated slope to the right indicates that the heart rules the head and the individual is emotionally motivated. This writer can be irresponsible, gushingly sentimental, sympathetic, and embarrassingly demonstrative. This person can be impulsive, has a need to relate to others, and can overdo everything so that he or she becomes physically exhausted.

Some positive keywords

active

adaptable

affectionate

curious

emotional

enterprising

progressive

sociable

sympathetic

trust in the future

Some negative keywords

accident-prone

easily distracted

excitable

forgetful

gregarious

gullible

hasty

hysterical

lack of discipline

too demonstrative

wasteful

THE VERTICAL OR UPRIGHT SLANT

a hot stove, you

Vertical or upright slant

The upright script indicates an independent person who is dominated by reason rather than emotions. People who display this trait are able to see both sides of an argument and they usually stay neutral. The closer the letters are to being upright, the more control these writers have over themselves. Completely vertical writing is a sign of poise, calm, self-reliance, and a neutral attitude to most things. These are mature, practical, and independent people whose heads rule their hearts. They can be self-sufficient; they have low emotional responses, and they can be restrained. These writers will not make a drama out of a crisis and they can be relied on in an emergency situation.

Some positive keywords

mature

prudent

analytical

independent

reserved

cautious

impartial

reliable

diplomatic

good self-control

an ability to concentrate

Some negative keywords

indifference

lack of emotional response

self-centered

critical observation

inactivity

a pessimistic outlook

THE LEFT SLANT

For that book. I would have come however, unfortunately there was

Left-handed slant

People whose handwriting slants to the left may be inclined to daydream, living an active inner life. They tend to be shy and reserved, and they are socially cautious. They can be observant, though, and can be good listeners. They are self-reliant and they don't intrude on the privacy of others. Some-one who writes with a left-handed slant, depending on the degree of slant, may have had a dominant mother figure during childhood. Perhaps the father was a weaker character, or possible he was totally absent. Such writers find comfort in behaving in an unconventional way and some find it hard to cope with change. If their handwriting displays an exaggerated left slant, they can have a morbid curiosity about death, may suffer inner rebellion, or they may be emotionally repressed.

Some positive keywords

persistent

sentimental

tender and devoted

Some negative keywords

fear of commitment

forced behavior

obstinacy

insecurity

insincerity

fussy

selfish

pedantic

overcautious

living in the past and fearing the future

curbed spontaneity

VARYING SLANT

"Journey of a Lifetime" Project, with the help of members of the Johann Strauss Society, I

Varying slant

Writers who have fluctuating and varying slants show versatility and an erratic streak; they can be impatient, intelligent, and highly active. This is also the writing of an unpredictable individual with changing behavior patterns who can experience mood swings and self-conflict. People with this handwriting characteristic like to mix and communicate with others; they enjoy variety and change in their lives; and they can be happy-go-lucky characters. This type of writing is often found in teenagers when they are unsettled, with all kinds of conflicting thoughts and ideas, and a need for social and emotional acceptance, and more independence.

Some positive keywords
adaptable
friendly
intelligent
versatile

Some negative keywords
inner conflict
neurosis
unpredictable
unstable

So far we have considered the slant of the writer; and knowing that a signature represents our public image, the way we write represents how we are feeling privately. Let us apply this concept to a few cases. You may wish to refer to Chapter 12, "The Signature: The Public Image."

LEFT-SLANT WRITING WITH A RIGHT-SLANT SIGNATURE

Left slant with right slant signature

Individuals who write with a left-handed slant but whose signatures have a right-handed slant value their privacy. They are reserved individuals who give the appearance of being outgoing. You can be sure that inside they are not nearly as spontaneous and outgoing as they appear to be.

STRONG RIGHT-SLANT WRITING WITH A VERTICAL SIGNATURE

Strong right slant writing with a vertical signature

Writers with a strong right-hand slant and an upright signature can have intense personalities, but they give the impression of being analytical and reserved. They have learned to control their intense nature in the public eye, but as you get to know them a little better, you will get to see this other side of them.

SMALL VERTICAL WRITING WITH A LARGE RIGHT-SLANT SIGNATURE

If you would like a magazine post you one. I like the   Man

Small vertical writing with large right slant signature

An individual who has small vertical writing but a large right-slant signature has an analytical mind, displays good attention to detail, has an image of a commanding presence, and has good interpersonal skills. Although people with this handwriting appear to be outgoing and socially very comfortable, inside they are reserved and private.

See how easy it is to combine handwriting traits to understand people better? Remember, we are looking at only a few traits, and there may be other aspects of an individual's handwriting that need to be included. Each trait is a piece of the picture!

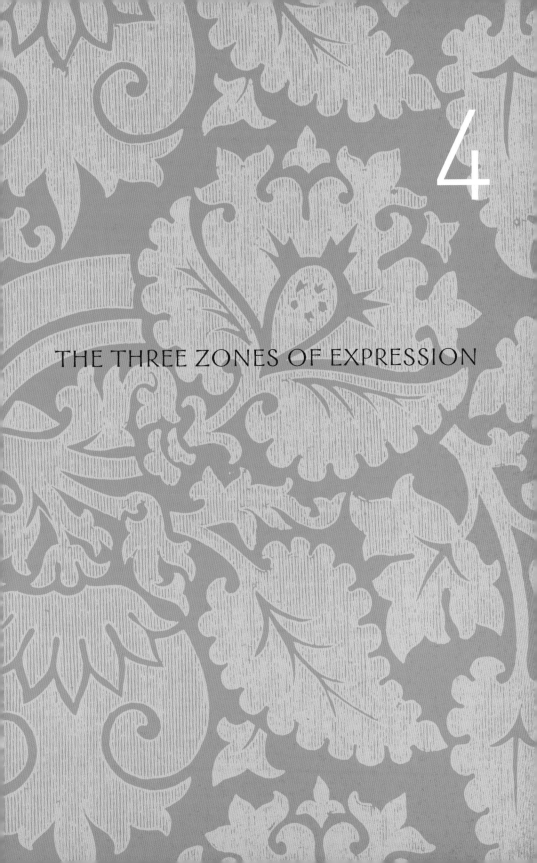

4

THE THREE ZONES OF EXPRESSION

The three zones of expression are the upper, middle, and lower zones. Where there is a lack of proportion or equality among the different zones, the dominant zones will point to the writer's overenthusiastic response in that area. Ideally, all three zones of handwriting should be balanced, showing a well-proportioned script; this scenario signifies the individual who is capable of leading a balanced life.

UPPER
MIDDLE
LOWER

Three zones

THE UPPER ZONE

The upper zone is the area that is covered by the stems of letters such as the lowercase letters *d* and *t* and all the capital letters. The upper extensions of the loops of the lowercase letters *b*, *f*, *h*, *k*, and *l* can be written in varying degrees of size and height. The top or upper zone reveals idealism, spiritual aspirations, ambitions, and intellect, plus the practicalities of life.

The maturity of an individual can be seen in the size of his or her writing in the upper and lower zones: the mature writer shows no exaggeration in either zone.

Loops Too High in the Upper Zone

If the loops in the upper zone are too high, the individual may be aiming too high in his or her search for perfection, and that the subject's idealistic qualities can lack realistic purpose.

Loops too high in the upper zone

46

Loops Too Small in the Upper Zone

Too small or nonexistent upper loops can be an indication of being too matter-of-fact and may suggest a lack of goals in life; this trait also indicates that logic and intellect take priority over emotion.

address letters
address of

Loops too small in the upper zone

Oversized Upper Loops

The writer of oversized upper loops displays a muddled mind, an exaggerated ego, and a tendency to show off and demand attention. This trait can also reveal an individual who shows signs of fantasy and of being a daydreamer; this writer can substitute the imaginary world for reality.

To focus

Oversized loops with the upper zone

Overwriting of Upper Loops

The person who retraces upper loops several times is revealing signs of insecurity and an indication of neurosis. He or she needs to make achievements but may be unable to do much or may be afraid to go forward for fear of making mistakes. This trait can also symbolize the gap between achievement and aspirations, particularly if the loops are oversized.

Kindly send
Register

Upper loops repeated in the upper zone

Thin and Narrow Loops in the Upper Zone

find my new address above.

Thin and narrow loops in the upper zone

If the upper-zone loops are too lean and narrow, the writer is either frustrated and restricted or perhaps too rational in his or her thinking. There can be religious leanings, or the absence of physical contact, and a lack of warmth within the family circle when the writer was a child, which prevents the individual from expressing his or her feelings. Thin and narrow loops are an indication of a lack of forward vision, a lack of perception, and stunted warmth.

Fuller Loops in the Upper Zone

could you provide

Fuller loops in the upper zone

Fuller loops in the upper zone indicate that the writer is imaginative, friendly, affectionate, and loving. This trait can also reveal liberal sentiments and emotional responses; individuals with this writing style like to express their feelings within friendships and close relationships.

Loops Sloping to the Left in the Upper Zone

they are not all of them some I have thrown in, the waste paper bin

Loops sloping to the left, in the upper zone

The writer who displays loops sloping to the left of the page within the upper zone can be showing an active inner life,

48

including the traits of contemplation and a tendency to brood on memories and experiences. This writing shows introverted tendencies.

Loops Sloping to the Right in the Upper Zone

Loops sloping to the right, in the upper zone

Loops that slope toward the right of the page within the upper zone can indicate intellectual ambitions. The person who shows this writing trait has a lot of drive and energy, with the desire to use his or her mental abilities in a constructive way. The individual whose writing slopes to the right is usually an extrovert.

Varying Sizes of Loops in the Upper Zone

A handwriting sample with a variety of sizes displayed in the loops of the upper zone, sometimes fluctuating in length and width, can reveal the writer's tendency to vary his or her moods. This individual's ideas and ambitions suffer accordingly, and he or she may be optimistic one day, pessimistic the next.

Fluctuating sizes of loops in the upper zone

THE MIDDLE ZONE

The middle zone of handwriting reveals whether the writer is a "thinking" or a "feeling" type of person. Letters within the middle zone show whether the writer offers warmth and affection in relationships or prefers to take an analytical and logical approach. This zone can also show the social attitude of the writer.

The middle zone is the area where all lowercase letters without loops are formed; it represents a balance between the upper and lower zones. All lowercase letters should be written at the same height.

The middle zone concerns social life, the emotions, practical behavior, and everyday life. It can show the things that motivate the individual. It shows how someone adapts to circumstances both on a mental and emotional level. Children's writing has a large middle zone.

Very large middle zone writing

Very Large Writing in the Middle Zone

A very large script in the middle zone shows that the writer can be self-absorbed; although this individual can be socially outgoing and friendly, he or she can also be egotistical. Such writers might overreact to people and events. Someone whose writing is large in the middle zone area can be generous and extravagant. This trait also shows that this writer can enjoy him- or herself on a grand scale, to the extent of going over the top. Although apparently confident, this person might actually be hiding self-consciousness.

Inflated or exaggerated middle-zone writers tend to be somewhat immature in their emotional attitude and can be highly sensitive to any form of personal criticism.

Large Writing in the Middle Zone

last communication

Large middle zone writing

Large middle-zone writers are aware of other people and thrive on being the center of attention and in the thick of a social gathering, such as a party. They love attention and dislike being in the background. Also, a capital letter inserted in the middle zone indicates that the writer seeks acknowledgement and has a desire for recognition. Occasionally, such a capital letter appears in the handwriting of artistic or creative people who want to appear more clever and interesting than they really are. The capital letters that occur most frequently in the middle zone are *R* and *M*.

Small Writing in the Middle Zone

*Would it be possible
you to send me some*

Small middle zone writing

Writers with a small middle zone are thinkers who use an analytical approach to solve the problems of love and life.

Such writers usually keep their emotions in check and do not tend to act impulsively or rashly. These people are usually happiest being observers, and they can be less spontaneous than most in their friendships. They tend to hold back on introductions and they do not always trust people.

THE LOWER ZONE

The lower zone is the area where the traits of physical health, sexual drive, materialistic concerns, and instinctive behavior are seen. This zone is where you find the lower loops of the lowercase script letters *f, g, j, p, q, y,* and *z.* Here the personality traits are governed by the length and width of the loops.

The lower zone in handwriting reveals the sexual instincts of the writer; the way the lowercase letters *g* and *y* are formed gives the clues to the writer's attitudes and preferences. Whether these letters are written with or without loops, with heavy pressure or light, can reveal quite a lot about the writer's materialistic drives and energy levels. The correct way of writing a *g* or *y* is to bring the stroke down, around, and up, crossing over to form a loop.

There are many variations of the loop, and this is where the signs of inhibition, vanity, sensuality, sexuality, and material-ism are revealed.

Long, Rounded Loops with Pressure in the Lower Zone

A very long, rounded loop with plenty of pressure within the lower zone is a sign of energy and drive, but also strong sexual inclinations and a need for the writer to express them. This can also show that the writer is fond of playing sports, especially team games.

Long rounded loop with pressure in lower zone

Thin, Wavering Slopes in the Lower Zone

A thin, wavering down stroke or loop in the lower zone indicates a lack of vitality, energy, or interest in life.

Thin, wavering down stroke, in lower zone

Short, Rounded Loops in the Lower Zone

Short loops, rounded and full at base

A loop in the lower zone that is short and full with a round base shows a love of flirting and an affectionate and loving nature, but not necessarily a sensual or sexy one. This type of writer will probably enjoy the chase much more than the capture.

Inflated Loops in the Lower Zone

An exaggerated *g* or *y* in the lower zone with an inflated loop shows that the writer can be boastful; this trait can also indicate an inflated ego. Writers with this trait are apt to brag about their sexuality and they love to be the center of attention. Often they are compensating for an inferiority complex, and their feelings are superficial and are not supported by a great deal of action.

Exaggerated *y* with inflated loop

Loops Leaning to the Left in the Lower Zone

Lower zone loop leaning to the left

Loops leaning to the left in the lower zone can indicate a mother fixation. This trait is often seen in the writing of men who find it hard to establish relationships with the opposite sex. This trait can also indicate a person still living at home, probably looking after a mother or caring for an elderly person whose health is poor.

Loops Leaning to the Right in the Lower Zone

Lower zone loop leaning to the right

Loops in the lower zone that lean to the right are an indication of a strong father influence in the writer's early and formative years.

Lines Instead of Loops in the Lower Zone

Lower zone loop leaning to the right

A simple line rather than a loop within the lower zone reveals good concentration skills and business acumen. It can also show a tendency to neglect instinctive drives or intuition. This writer channels a lot of energy into work and career, inhibiting natural emotional needs.

Long, Unlooped Downward Strokes

A long, unlooped downward stroke going right is an indication of an interest in psychic subjects and psychology.

Long, unlooped downward stroke

5

THE BASELINE

The baseline is one of the most important areas of handwriting. We are instructed as children to observe the baseline and to write in straight lines. The reality is, however, that even after years of practice, few people can actually write in a straight line on unlined paper.

The baseline shows how well an individual is handling stress at the time of writing and it can be an indicator of the writer's mood at any one time. Deviations from writing in a perfectly straight line are normal.

NORMAL, STRAIGHT BASELINE

I think being a parent is a very hard job especially to teenagers,

Straight baseline

People who write with a normal, straight baseline are reliable and determined individuals who are self-motivated and self-controlled. They are orderly, methodical, and responsible and have strong minds that control their emotions. A person who writes in a straight line is not usually deterred from his or her aims and goals. If a person writes precisely in a straight line, then we may say that person is unyielding.

ASCENDING OR RISING BASELINE

send me your brochure on astrology courses etc,

Rising baseline

Baselines that ascend in steps are often found in the handwriting of those who have little stamina. Writers of this type of baseline are usually optimistic and ambitious and have a positive attitude; they are willing to cooperate with others, and they tend to emphasize the positive view. They have a strong response to new ideas.

DESCENDING OR FALLING BASELINE

Best wishes to you all for the New Year

Falling baseline

A descending or falling baseline usually indicates someone who is overworked, is suffering from fatigue, and has too much to do in a short space of time. Tired and overwhelmed, this individual tends to have a pessimistic attitude and can be depressive. A baseline that descends in steps is often found in writers who bravely fight off depressive moods. This trait is also indicative of an older person's writing, and it can indicate ailments such as arthritis or osteoporosis, or depression and fatigue. Aching bones and arm muscles that become weak and drop toward the body cause this writing. Grief and emotional pain show here, but this can be of a temporary nature.

WAVY OR ERRATIC BASELINE

Please can you send me a copy of your prospectus I am from

Erratic baseline

Wavy or erratic baselines may be indicative of moodiness. Teenagers often write with this kind of baseline when they are unsettled, with their minds and moods all over the place due to hormonal changes and a lack of definite direction in life. People who write with an erratic baseline can be emotionally unsettled, unpredictable, unstable, and indecisive.

6

SPACING

Spacing is a little more complex than other facets of handwriting. The following guidelines regarding spacing are based generally upon accepted principles of graphology. As with all other traits and indications in handwriting, spacing must be considered in relation to other factors in the handwriting sample. There are three basic elements of spacing relating to handwriting: spacing between the words, spacing between the letters, and spacing between the lines. The distance between the letters and words is difficult to alter at will when an individual is writing at normal speed. Spacing between the lines, however, is a matter of choice, which a person with average mentality can alter when writing at normal speed. For reasons of available space or personal taste, therefore, the amount of space that appears between the lines is likely to be an indication of conscious preference.

SPACING BETWEEN WORDS

"Cursive" is another word for running script or joined-up writing. Good handwriting is based on a pattern of parallel lines and ovals. Normal spacing between words should be a gap the size of one lowercase letter *o*. A capital letter should start on the baseline and reach no higher than the top of the loop in a lowercase letter such as an *h*. A letter that finishes in the upper part of the middle zone should join the next letter horizontally, and a letter finishing in the lower part of the middle zone should join the next letter diagonally.

Word spacing can be related to the way in which we speak. When a person speaks with intermittent pauses, it may be because he or she is accustomed to pondering and considering before acting. It can also be because the person wants to let his or her words be understood by the listener. However, if the pauses outweigh the importance of the speech, then we may conclude that the speaker is conceited.

Even Spacing between Words

but being a lawyer
the Code you sent me

Even spacing between the words

The spaces between words can reflect how a writer relates to others. If the spacing is neat and even, the writer usually enjoys the company of others and tends to have a genuine concern for his or her fellow human beings. The writer whose handwritten script is regular and flowing normally leaves the correct amount of spacing between the words; the writing is neither too crowded nor too far apart. Most secretaries leave the correct spacing between words in their handwriting, having used a typewriter or word processor for many years.

Wide Spacing between Words

enough to send me a list of recommended

Wide spacing between the words

Wide spacing between words is an indication that the writer is not too friendly and prefers his or her own company. These individuals need privacy and distance from others. Widely spaced words are associated with intelligent and independent leaders. These writers take time and effort to think through problems carefully before making a decision. Individuals with this style of writing can be critical and argumentative. When a writer's words are sometimes widely spaced and at other times narrowly set apart, then we may say that this individual is unstable in both thinking and emotions.

Little Spacing between Words

Little space between the words

up, using my day, month, year, to find out if there are any which I could use to better

A person who writes with little spacing between the words may have a lot to say for him- or herself but says little of any importance. If there are no spaces between the writer's words, this is indicative of a person of action. This person can also be impulsive. He or she may seek constant contact and closeness with others and have strong feelings of inse-curity. The writer can also be introverted and self-conscious and suffer from personal inhibition.

SPACING OF LETTERS WITHIN WORDS

Long Joining Extensions within Words

An individual who writes with long joining extensions within words shows a lack of inhibitions and is usually an extrovert. These people are considerate and sensitive to those around them. It is important, however, that these writers have time to themselves because they are generous and open-minded but often find it difficult to say no to friends and family, which can exhaust their own energies.

I understand

Long-joining extensions with the word

Narrow or Irregular Spacing within Words

Close and irregular spacing within words is indicative of a person who can talk nonstop on his or her chosen topic. This trait often is characteristic of people who are impatient but loyal. These individuals are practical and logical and can have good organizational skills. They can be specialists in their chosen field of work, but they have few interests outside their careers. Writers whose letters are all narrowly spaced within the words are usually introverted and cautious. They generally lack faith in their own abilities. Indeed, when they are in love, their insecurities can mean that they are prone to jealousy. Writers of this type of script can display self-consciousness, inhibitions, and introversion. Some of these individuals have a fear of loneliness and crave contact with people but have little or no respect for the privacy of others.

What is happening to set any markings

Irregular spacing within the words

SPACING BETWEEN LINES

The space between the lines is most probably deliberately planned and can be described as the picture of the writer's mind. Lines of writing should have enough space between them so the upward and downward strokes do not touch.

Large Spacing between Lines

What is happening
to set any markings

Large spacing between the lines

A person who writes with widely spaced lines may be said to live an ordered life. These people have executive ability and are reasonable in their thinking. If the space between the lines becomes too large, however, it may indicate that this is a person who likes to keep his or her distance. Large spacing between the lines can be an indication that the writer is out of contact with others. Individuals who write this way desperately need love and affection, but they are afraid to get too involved in an intimate relationship for fear of getting hurt. This can also be due to a fear of failure in a shy, withdrawn, and emotional person. This spacing can also be indicative of writers who are out of touch with the realities of everyday life. Although they can be distrusting of others, they fear isolation. The distance between the words indicates the extent of this person's solitude.

Normal Spacing between Lines

like some of your booklets and information on your courses,

Normal spacing between the lines of writing

Normal or "copybook" spacing between the written lines belong to someone who thinks clearly and who has inner balance and harmony, sound judgment and a sense of proportion.

Cramped Spacing between Lines

up, using my day, month, year, to find out if there are any which I could use to better

Cramped spacing between the lines

Small spacing between the lines may indicate a person who likes to be around other people. Script with cramped spacing between the lines, with the bottom loops on one line mixing with the upper loops of the next line, is an indication of a person with muddled mind who needs contact with others. This trait is also an indication of confusion for this writer, who lacks perspective and has poor judgment.

7

CONNECTIONS AND FORMATION
OF THE LETTERS

The way we connect the letters in script, or fail to do so, can reveal the way we think and our attitude toward others. It can also tell us whether we rely more on the logical mind or on intuitive faculties when finding solutions to problems. The two factors that need consideration are the way that letters are formed and the way they connect to one another.

The connection and formation styles fall into six categories: copybook, arcade, angular, garland, wavy-line, and thread-like. There are also four common letter styles: artistic, artificial, simple, and copybook. The degree of connection between letters takes two forms. In the first form, most of the letters are joined together to form a continuous active movement, which promotes a fluent and lively pace. In the second, the letters are joined in varying amounts and ways.

CONNECTED LETTERS

Love been told to

Connected letters

People who write with "joined up" letters are logical and well organized. They see the logical order in which to do things and they solve problems in a practical manner. Their conversation flows easily and they mix well with others because they understand relationships. Some people go the extreme of joining up actual words as well as letters, because they don't want to lose their train of thinking while they are writing. Such people may find writing something of a strain.

Some positive keywords

adaptability

consistency

deductive thinking

good memory

logical mind

sociability

Some negative keywords

inclined to reach hasty conclusions

inconsiderateness

superficiality

DISCONNECTED LETTERS

information and an

Disconnected letters

In disconnected script, usually no more than three letters are connected to each other in one word. This type of hand-writing can point to a thought process influenced by intuition or to a lack of concentration. The writer who does not join letters concentrates on details rather than the whole project. This type of handwriting might be typical of a supervisor who ignores all that you have achieved but picks on the one mistake you've made. This trait can also indicate a writer who comes up with original ideas. Those who write with a disconnected script are influenced by their intuition and they find it difficult to ignore. These writers prefer to keep their distance from others. They can put a barrier around themselves and do not like the close company of others. Because they choose to behave this way, they can suffer loneliness, but they do not display it. These imaginative people channel their inventiveness into an artistic outlet.

Some positive keywords

cautious

imaginative

independent

individualistic

intuitive thinkers

inventive

self-reliant

creative

musical

artistic

Some negative keywords

lack of forethought

lonely

moody

stubborn

uncooperative

unreliable

unsociable

FORMS OF CONNECTION

There are six basic letter formations in graphology: copybook, arcade, angular, garland, wavy-line, and threadlike. Each of these styles reveals a different personality trait, and these styles are of great importance within handwriting analysis. When in school, we are taught to join our letters with rounded "copybook" connections. Some people retain this particular style, but others find their own connections. The writer's own individual personality is revealed within these formation styles.

Copybook Formation

send me an up to dat

Copybook style of script

Copybook style is taught rigorously in schools. It is the style of more conventional writers, those who have not, as yet, developed a way of thinking for themselves or a personality beyond that of their school days. These writers feel safe by conforming to prescribed and accepted patterns of thought and structured behavior with little or no originality. Some people writing in this style may come from a poor educational background.

This style is rarely used alone because it usually appears within a mixture of styles. It can be used deliberately, for the purpose of disguise (as in anonymous letters). Nuns, nurses, priests, and devoted teachers can write in this way, but don't forget that this style can also hide criminal tendencies.

Some positive keywords

conventional

predictable

Some negative keywords

criminal tendencies

deliberate

slow

lack of originality

not easy to motivate

orthodox habits

Arcade Formations

please send me details

Arcade connections

The writing of someone who uses the arcade style of script is humped and rounded at the top of the middle zone. The writer of arcade-type script shows a more formal way of styling letters and this indicates that he or she has a traditional sense of values. These individuals are not ones for making instant friendships, as they like to evaluate situations and people before committing themselves. An individual who uses arcade script often is creative; possible tendencies are toward musical talent or having an eye for shape and color. People who write in this style prefer to keep their own counsel and rarely let others know their true thoughts and feelings until they know them well. These writers can mix and communicate well with others when necessary, although they like to keep their personal lives private.

Arcade writers can be staid in their ways and rigid in their thinking. They have their own set of rules from which they operate, and nothing can deter them from their way of doing things, which is the conventional way. Teachers often have this type of writing, as do architects. The *m*'s and *n*'s within the script can be arch shaped.

Some positive keywords

cautious

confidentiality

constructive

conventionality

formal manners

loyalty

retentive memory

security

trustworthiness

Some negative keywords

close-minded

distrustful

hypocritical

lack of personality and imagination

secretive

stubborn

Angular Formations

all these years

Angular connections

Angular connections in the middle zone show an analytical mind; the sharp points give the impression of probing. The angular writer is persistent and he doesn't back away from difficult tasks. Individuals with this style of writing have an intelligent approach and self-discipline and they are willing to work hard in a situation that needs constant attention to detail. The writer whose script is angular displays individuality; the lines are sharp and sometimes even pointed, particularly the tops of the lowercase *m*'s and *n*'s.

People who use this style of writing are shrewd individuals who have a practical and down-to-earth approach. The writer of angular script is critical of others, and if the writer also presses down hard on the page, this can be an indication of aggression. These writers are observant people who are able to concentrate on details. People with large angular writing can be self-centered and possibly lack tolerance for the opinions and ideas of others. An individual with the angular style of writing can be prone to cutting remarks without thought for the other person's feelings. This writer tends to learn by his or her own mistakes.

Some positive keywords
creative thinking

determined

ethical

hardworking

objective

reliable

Some negative keywords

argumentative

conflict

cruelty

hard

obstinate

irritable

lack of compromise

resistant to others' ideas

sadism

sharp

tense

Garland Formations

can you send me

Garland connections

Garland script is easily and quickly formed and is usually the script of people who are prone to laziness. They are, however, kind, friendly, and affectionate individuals who do not have aggression in their nature; they prefer harmony to friction in their lives. These people like an active social life and they enjoy the company of friends and family. This person is an excellent host, who enjoys entertaining on a grand scale. The person who uses the garland style of writing is also a "Dear Abby," to whom people are drawn in order to pour out their troubles. People with this writing style are expressive and cooperative and are usually at ease with most people and the environment; they normally avoid conflict. These writers are not competitors; they will compromise by taking the path of least resistance. Some of these individuals are open to emotional influence and can be gullible.

Some positive keywords

adjustability

friendliness

kindness

lack of formality

optimistic outlook

receptiveness

Some negative keywords

complacent

gullible

laziness

tactless

talkative

thoughtlessness

weakness

Wavy-Line Formations

to have fun and learn the

Wavy-line connections

Writers who use wavy-line formations need freedom to adapt to circumstances and the environment. They do not easily commit themselves fully to any event; they prefer to keep their individuality without obligations. Their thinking is usually flighty and subjective, and they have no definite goals or pattern in life, preferring to ebb and flow with the tide.

Some positive keywords

go with the flow

diplomatic

freedom loving

Some negative keywords

avoiding commitment

two-faced

Threadlike Formations

The threadlike formation is like a length of thread laid out on the page, rather than letters being formed, as there is no real letter definition in the writing. Threadlike script is indicative of excellent manipulating ability. These people are mentally alert and difficult to pin down, and others find them particularly difficult to understand. These rest-

aromatherapy well as remedy

Threadlike connections

less and elusive writers can sometimes be inconsistent. They hate to be tied down to one course of action and like to be free to do their own thing rather than follow any set, structured routine. These individuals can understand other people and have an aptitude for getting their own way without too much trouble. The positive traits associated with this type of writer are that they are quick thinkers and intelligent individuals. On the negative side, these writers can be secretive, they may change facts to suit their own ends, and they can be confused.

The threadlike connection style is, in some instances, almost illegible. This style is often found at the end of a word that ends with -ing, which can be written as one final downward movement. Writers who use the threadlike formation have very strong instincts for self-preservation and they can adapt to any situation, provided it is to their advantage and without loss to their own individuality. If they do not have the freedom to pursue their creative abilities, they will balk at any confined convention. However, they prefer to follow a trouble-free path and avoid restrictions.

These writers have an instinctive, spontaneous understanding of others but can manipulate people to follow their own commands and ideas without being overbearing, and they do have likable personalities. People with this style of writing can be found in the field of psychology, where their strong powers of observation stand them in good stead. They can view both sides of a situation and give advice without being drawn into the situation themselves.

Another type of threadlike connection occurs when the thread is within the word; this connection can appear in any part of a word, and sometimes even throughout the word. In the most negative form of the threadlike connection, a word can be written as one letter followed by a line. Thread writers are indecisive and unsure of themselves, which leaves them open to influence. They find it difficult to cope with external pressures, which they find stressful. These people can be creative but prefer to learn by experience rather than formal training or teaching.

Some positive keywords

agile mind

broadminded

individual ideas

need for freedom

reliant on instinct

self-aware

versatile

Some negative keywords

avoid aggression

feelings of insecurity

hysterical

impressionable

unstable

FORMS OF LETTERS

There are four basic styles to the forms of letters: artistic, artificial, simple, and copybook. Some writers can reduce their basic form to the point of neglect, while others overemphasize with flourishes and embellishments. To be analyzed correctly, the sample of script should be legible, original, and spontaneously written.

Artistic Form of Letters

Yours Faithfully

Artistic form of letters

All The Best, Love, From

Writers who form artistic letters are usually intelligent and naturally artistic. They add ornamentation to their script but retain legibility by the natural way they form their letters.

Artificial form of letters

Artificial Form of Letters

Very florid and highly adorned and stylized script can belong to a person who is trying to hide an inferiority complex or to give the impression of being artistic or talented, while actually being nothing of the kind.

Simple Form of Letters

my new address

Simple form of letters

Writers who produce script that is stripped down to the bare essentials but that still retains legibility have active minds and aesthetic awareness. These writers prefer friends with whom they can have deep, meaningful discussions, and who can share their interests and intellectual interactions. Such writers can cut corners and simplify tasks to save time and effort. These writers would be unreliable in a situation that demands their concentration on minor details, as they would find it boring and become restless.

Copybook Form of Letters

to view a house,

Copybook form of letters

While this style of writing is "correct," there is little individuality, so writers using this form are lacking in imagination and originality. These writers are difficult to motivate; however, they are reliable in situations that require repetitive activity and they are content to stay within imposed restrictions, as their minds require little stimulus.

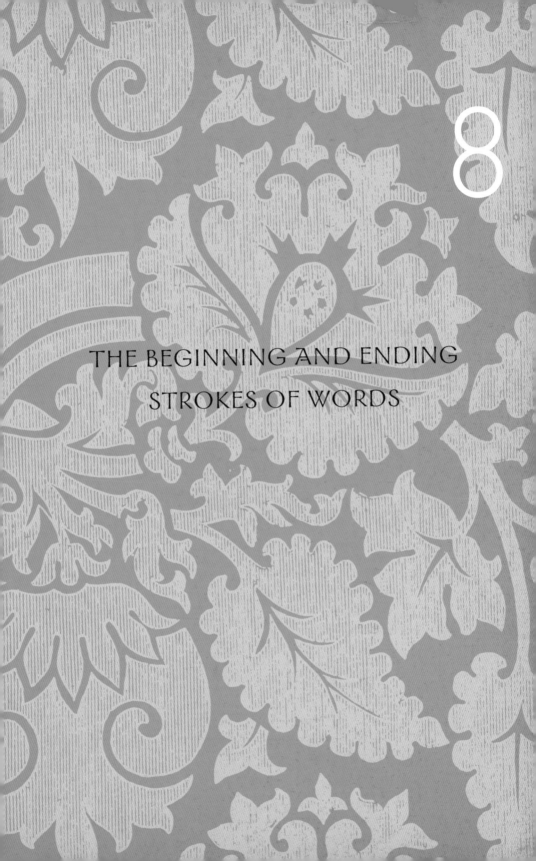

8

THE BEGINNING AND ENDING
STROKES OF WORDS

The strokes that are made by the writer at the beginning and at the end of each word need to be taken into consideration in any handwriting analysis, as this trait indicates the amount of preparation, if any, that this person requires before going into action. Whether the script is unnecessary or constructive will reveal whether the writer is likely to finish the task at hand.

THE INITIAL STROKES

As we were taught in elementary school, the writer creates the initial stroke at the beginning of each word written.

Long Initial Strokes

Long initial stroke on letters

Generally speaking, a long initial stroke shows that the writer needs time to make inner preparations before starting anything new. A combination of long initial strokes and a slow pace of writing suggest that the writer is dim-witted.

When an initial stroke is fairly long and the speed is decidedly fast, this signifies that the writer gets into the swing of things and maintains the rhythm of activity. A long starting stroke from below the baseline can act as a springboard, but the writing speed must be at least moderately fast for this to be considered a positive factor.

When there is a springboard stroke and the writing is slow, this can indicate that the writer is strongly relating to past ties, to a mother figure, and to the influences of early life experiences. A fast writer, however, is not affected too strongly by events in earlier years.

No Initial Stroke

more information regarding your organisation and the courses you

No initial stroke on letters

Writers who dive right in to their script without making initial strokes are unlikely to follow set patterns and methods. They are flexible and they can adapt to whatever circumstances they find themselves in. They are not fussy or careful and they ignore inessential details. They have a positive attitude to life.

Feeling Strokes

With love

Feeling strokes

The feeling stroke is another form of graphic hesitation. In this case, writers make a few faint starting marks, which may appear as leading strokes, while they are considering their subject and before they begin to write. These writers normally have a copybook style of script. They lack confidence and rarely achieve much because their hesitation and deliberation impede their efforts. The feeling stroke is rare, however, and it usually belongs to those who seldom need to write anything at all.

week by methods

Hooks on initial stroke

Hooks

This starting stroke can indicate constructive thinking and persistence. It can also, however, indicate an angry response to interruptions.

Initial Stroke Resting on the Baseline

the reviews to be late

Initial stroke resting on the baseline

When the initial stroke rests squarely on the baseline, the writer will take orders from those who are in positions of authority, follow regulations and conform to what is acceptable to others. When faced with a decision, these people may feel anxious and inadequate. They usually have a copybook form of script.

THE ENDING STROKES

The Letter *E*

the me the the

1. **Shows a liberal attitude to others and to change**
2. **Has a normal disposition to others**

3. **An indication of determination, curiosity, and suspicion**
4. **This can also be a sign of weakness and timidity**

The Letter *D*

Sen*d* interested send *Lend*

Ending strokes on the letter *d*

1. **This type of d can indicate an aggressive attitude**
2. **Can also be an obstinate individual who likes to be in control**
3. **Normal social attitude**
4. **This can show unemotional tendencies**

Most writers end their words with a tailing-off stroke, and these strokes can run from a long stroke to an abrupt ending. These tailing-off strokes relate to an interest in others and they may represent a kind of "reaching out" to others. Therefore, an abrupt ending can indicate a boring person or a lack of energy and drive. The lowercase letter *e* is the best letter to look at but the letter *d* is also interesting, as the writer needs to change direction to produce the end stroke before moving on to the next word.

9

PRESSURE

There are three types of pressure to be considered in handwriting: heavy, light, and medium. This pressure displays how much energy a writer has and how it is transformed into activity. It reveals whether the writer is a high-activity worker with an emotional nature, or a sensitive, rather highly strung individual with a lack of energy to fall back on. Turn the page over and look at the back and you will soon see whether the writing pressure is heavy or not.

HEAVY PRESSURE

not disappointed

Heavy pressure in handwriting

Heavy pressure indicates commitment and taking things seriously, but excessively heavy pressure signifies that these writers get very uptight at times and can react quickly to what they might see as criticism, even though none is intended. These individuals will react first and ask questions afterward. Heavy pressure in handwriting also indicates energy and drive—and sometimes aggression. These writers can be forceful in an argument. They are doers rather than thinkers but can be overemotional. Sometimes they are egotistical, with a strong need for materialistic success. These individuals enjoy eating and drinking, and they can have a high sexual drive. They prefer activity to contemplation and often like to work with their hands.

LIGHT PRESSURE

Light pressure reveals a sensitive personality and mental alertness, combined with a strong critical streak if the writing is angular. These writers can easily be hurt and may be bruised emotionally. They write with the minimum of energy and are not likely to be active and volatile, but they can be touchy when frustrated in their aims. They dislike unnecessary force or argument and have the ability to adapt to situations with subtle manipulation rather than hostility. These writers are quickly offended by words and often lack tolerance when ruffled; also, they can be sarcastic and irritable. Very light pressure can indicate spirituality, modesty, sensitivity to atmosphere, and empathy toward others, but it shows a lack of vitality. The writer who uses light pressure does not wish to dominate others.

Light pressure in handwriting

MEDIUM PRESSURE

Writers who use medium pressure show good balance between intellect and emotion. These writers are usually adaptable, and while they may not be as energetic or highly active as the heavy-pressure writer, they like to strike an even note in life and do not go to extremes. The majority of people use this level of pressure.

Medium pressure in handwriting

10

CAPITAL LETTERS

Capital letters can give many clues to one's personality and can prove an excellent guide to the ego structure of the writer. The capital letters can reveal self-esteem or an inferiority complex. Whether the capital letters are large or small, plain or adorned with flourishes, they can show the writer's true character.

TYPES OF CAPITAL LETTERS

Large capital letter

Large Capital Letters

Writers who use large capital letters tend to have an exaggerated opinion of themselves. If the capital letters are three times larger than the rest of the script, writers enjoy being noticed and love to show off and be the center of attention within their circle of friends. This handwriting trait indicates people who are flamboyant and who may think that they are highly sexed. They can be overpowering in social circles, and their desire to impress can cloud their judgment.

Small capital letter

Small Capital Letters

Small capital letters are a sign of an introspective nature and a retiring disposition. Individuals who use small capital letters can have feelings of inferiority and may shy away from the limelight, preferring to be part of the crowd. These writers need to be more assertive and to develop more drive if they are to succeed in life.

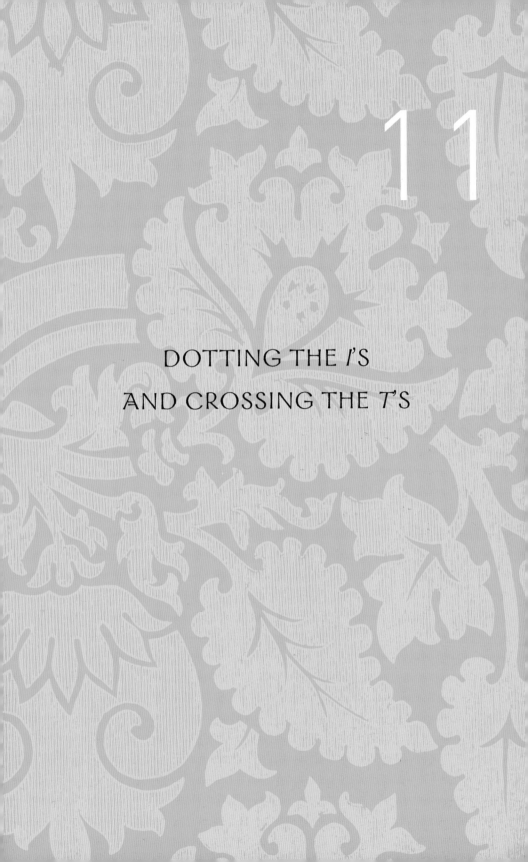

11

DOTTING THE *I*'S
AND CROSSING THE *T*'S

"Dotting the *i*'s and crossing the *t*'s" is an expression that most of us have heard in some context or other, but in the analysis of a handwriting sample, both these actions are very important. When we are writing, dotting our *i*'s and crossing our *t*'s is automatic; we don't really give any thought to the action.

CROSSING THE *T*

The way the writer places the bar across the stem of the letter *t* can indicate whether the individual is confident, ambitious, pessimistic, cautious, or spontaneous. However, this one indicator is not conclusive; one must also look at all the other indicators. The *t* bar should be evaluated according to:

Its location in relation to the downward stroke

The significance of rightward and leftward movement

Whether it is placed high or low on the stem

T bar connected to the following letter

T Bar Connected to the Following Letter

A *t* bar connected to the following letter can be a sign of writing speed and can denote an intelligent and quick mind.

T bar at left of stem

T Bar to the Left of the Stem

A *t* bar placed to the left of the stem can reveal caution and a tendency to hold back, particularly when the writer is making decisions. This person is too cautious, so he or she can miss opportunities as a result of this.

Ornately Decorated Underline

People who decorate the underline under their signatures find themselves fascinating and they are particularly concerned with their appearance. They may act or speak in an artificial manner to impress others.

Ornately decorated underline

Short, Light Underline

Short and light underline

A short underline created with light pressure is showing a lack of drive and energy.

Several Underlines

A signature with several strokes to the underline can denote a self-assertive, overbearing, uncompromising individual.

Several strokes underlined

Two Different Underlines

The writer who has two different types of strokes underlining his or her signature is displaying a great need for attention. This individual may use an assumed manner of speech, dress, or behavior to impress others.

Crossed strokes underlining a name can indicate a sign of anger or a sarcastic streak. This writer does not suffer fools gladly and likes to be seen as a dominant individual.

Two different strokes underlined

MIXED WRITING

Small Writing, Large Signature

I hope you all have a marvellous time in Fuerteventura.

Small writing and large signature

People with small writing and a large signature are expending significant energy on overcoming the conflict between their private, quiet nature and a need to be noticed. The gap in the size, from small writing to a large signature, indicates a big difference between the way such people feel inside—as private individuals—and how they present themselves—as people who get attention.

Small Writing, Small Signature

draw to a close here and brings a full recovery

M. Jane

Small writing and small signature

Small writing accompanied by a small signature is often characteristic of a person who has good concentration skills but who also can be introverted. People whose handwriting is small and who have a small signature pay particular attention to minute details, so care should be taken to ensure that all the facts are at hand when working with them.

Medium Writing, Large Signature

Hello,
Please send me information about correspondence courses.

Thanks
(R.J. Sprockett.

Medium size writing with a large signature

It is not unusual for people to sign their name a little larger than they normally write. This characteristic is a very common writing trait, and it is an indication that they are making an effort to be noticed.

Medium Writing, Small Signature

Happy New Year.

Fred etc.

Medium size writing with a large signature

A person whose signature is smaller than the accompanying text can be displaying inhibition, timidity, meanness, or unsatisfactory attitudes at home.

conclusion

Now that we have covered the basics of handwriting analysis, let us see how a professional might use the system. Here is the story of two women who answered an advertisement for a job.

Two ladies are waiting to be interviewed by a specialist at their local hospital. They have been short-listed to attend an interview for the post of personal assistant. Part of the job description is to communicate with patients in person, by letter, and on the telephone, regarding appointments and general inquiries. In terms of qualifications and experience, there is little difference between the two applicants, as they have both worked in busy medical practices for a number of years.

Faced with the challenge of choosing between the two candidates, the specialist gives a sample of each woman's handwriting to a graphologist for analysis. Both candidates are married, and they are both in their forties. To distinguish between them, we will call candidate A Beryl and candidate B Joan. By reading through the analyses of the two handwriting samples, it should be possible to ascertain which candidate was selected for the position.

Please forward the relevant literature for the courses.

Beryl's handwriting

Beryl's sample reveals evenly spaced margins with a slight right-handed slant, and her script is of medium size, with her small letters predominantly in the middle zone. Her baseline is relatively straight, and the spacing between her words is neat and even. Also, the distance between the lines is basically normal. Her letters are mostly connected and her style of writing is garland.

This sample shows a woman that has good planning skills. She is friendly and has an outgoing disposition, and she enjoys human contact. Her social instincts are well developed and she can leave her ego aside and focus on others when she interacts with them. Beryl is practical, flexible, and adaptable and has good organizational abilities. She is a thinking person who keeps her own emotions in check. She is orderly, methodical, and responsible and feels genuine concern for her fellow human beings. She is a clear thinker with inner balance and harmony, and she has a logical approach to solving problems as they arise. This woman's writing reveals that she is expressive, cooperative, and usually at ease with most people and with the environment, and she normally avoids conflict.

I have been too snowed-under to study but I really do want to start at some point!

Joan's handwriting

Joan's handwriting sample shows a wide upper margin with a more pronounced right-handed slant. Her script is small, and most of the letters are within the middle zone. The base-line is descending, and her words are widely spaced. Also, her letters are narrowly divided within the words, and her style of writing is arcade.

Joan's writing shows that she is respectful of her employer and elders and tends to live in the present, with little thought for the future. She can be irresponsible and overly sentimental. Although she is sympathetic, she can be embarrassingly demonstrative. She has a tendency to ana-lyze everything, including her thoughts and feelings. She is a thinking person, and she uses an analytical approach to the problems of life. Her writing indicates that she can be prone to fatigue if she is overworked and that she is unable to labor under pressure. This tendency can lead to a pes-simistic attitude, and she can become depressive. Although her writing shows intelligence and independence, she may take time and effort to think through her problems carefully before making a decision. She has a tendency to be intro-verted and overly cautious, and she lacks faith in her own abilities. Joan prefers to keep her own counsel, and she rarely lets others know her true thoughts and feelings, at least until she has worked them out for herself. She can mix and communicate well with others when necessary, although she likes to keep her personal life private.

Which candidate do you think was offered the position? Given the requirements of the job, it is quite understandable that candidate A was the successful applicant.

keywords

Keyword	Indicators or traits
Adventurous	Right-slanted handwriting; broad, large upper and lower zones; firm pressure on page and narrow right-hand margin
Ambitious	Large writing with rising lines and firm pressure; large middle and upper zones; large signature with a strong rising *t* bar placed high on the stem
Amiable and adaptable	Medium-sized writing of average width with flowing, harmonious rhythm; rounded letters and garlands
Business acumen	Large lower zone; letters mainly connected but some disconnected; right forward slant; threadlike writing with mixed connections or angles; broad, medium, or large size; no right margin
Calm and poised	Upright or slightly left-handed slant to regular writing; rounded letterforms with straight lines and regular spacing

Careless	Irregular threadlike handwriting; letters broken with bodies incomplete
Cold natured	Left-handed slant to script with narrow and sharp strokes; angular letter connections and words widely spaced
Conventional	Copybook connections; writing medium-size to small; straight lines; upright or slight right-handed slant with balanced zones and regular spacing; letters connected
Decisive	Angular connections; regular writing; careful letter-forms
Economical	Narrow, small writing without any end strokes to letters; no margins whatsoever
Efficient	Regular handwriting with angular or copybook connections; carefully formed letters with *i* dots and *t* bars accurately placed
Extravagant	Large, broad writing with wide left margin; large spaces between words and lines

Extrovert personality	Large, broad writing with a right-handed slant; large middle-zone words close together, with all spaces filled
Fiery tempered	Forward right-slant with heavy pressure and angular connections; fierce, pointed, or thickened t bars and hooked starting strokes, or script starting from well below the baseline
Generous	Broad handwriting and large garland end-stroke letters
Good judgment	Clear, regular, legible, medium-size handwriting with upright or slight forward-slant connected letters; straight lines and margins
Imaginative	Large, broad handwriting; letters disconnected; large upper and lower zones with full loops to script and irregular writing
Indecisive	Threadlike connections; broad, irregular handwriting with lack of definition to letterforms

Inferiority complex	Small, narrow handwriting with light pressure and left-handed slant; descending lines, small signature, and small personal pronoun *I*
Introvert personality	Small, narrow handwriting with light pressure and left-handed slant; small middle zone and words wide apart with spaces left vacant
Modest	Small handwriting, small signature, small personal pronoun *I*, and small upper and middle zones to letters
Obtrusive	Very broad writing with firm pressure and angular connections
Optimistic	Rising lines with a dynamic, lively stroke and rounded letterforms; signature clear and rising, placed to center or right-hand side
Pessimistic	Falling lines and falling words with angular connections and broken letterforms; signature crossed through or placed to the left
Precise	Regular handwriting with straight lines and margins; letters clearly and meticulously formed with angular connections; accurate placing of *i* dots and *t* bars

Secretive	Handwriting completely connected, with arcades or copybook vowels such as *o* tightly looped and sealed; cover strokes retracing letters
Self-confident	Large, regular handwriting with large middle zone; upright or slight forward slant; large signature and large pronoun *I*
Self-disciplined	Regular handwriting; straight lines and margins with even word spacing; balanced zones with upright or slight slant
Sensual	Thick, indistinct stroke; broad handwriting but narrow word spacing; large lower zone to letters
Sociable	Broad, legible handwriting with harmonious rhythm; forward right-slant and words close together; large middle zone; letters connected with garlands; rounded letterforms
Tactful and diplomatic	Medium-size or small handwriting of average width with rounded letterforms and even pressure; garlands, arcades, or mixed connections; upright or slight forward-slant; words decreasing in size with wide spaces between them

Talkative	Large, broad handwriting connected with garlands; words and lines close together
Timid	Upright or left handed-slant; narrow, cramped letterforms, light pressure, and wide right margin
Unpredictable	Changing slant, irregular handwriting, and varying connections
Versatile	Irregular handwriting with some letters connected and others disconnected; rhythmic, flowing, and varying letterforms with threads, garlands, or arcades
Warm natured	Broad handwriting with a pasty, thick stroke, rounded letterforms, and words close together; right-handed slant

index